Birth. from the

O'Brien Publishers

WITTICISMS OF
OSCAR WILDE

WARNER MEMORIAL LIBRARY
EASTERN COLLEGE
ST. DAVIDS, PA. 19087

Witticisms of
OSCAR WILDE

COMPILED BY
DEREK STANFORD

Published in the United States
by DUFOUR EDITIONS, INC.
Chester Springs, Pa. 19425

JOHN BAKER
5 Royal Opera Arcade
Pall Mall, London SW1

© 1971 Derek Stanford
John Baker Publishers Ltd
5 Royal Opera Arcade
Pall Mall, London SW1

SBN 212 98394 6

PR 5812 .S65
Wilde, Oscar, 1854-1900.
Witticisms of Oscar Wilde;

Printed in Great Britain by
Clarke, Doble & Brendon Ltd
Plymouth

Circulation Count: 0

Worldcat Libraries: 27

Additional info:

To
ROBERT *and* AILEEN NYE

CONTENTS

COMPILER'S PREFACE	9
The Written Word	19
VICE, SIN AND VIRTUE	19
WOMEN AND MARRIAGE	21
LOVE, FRIENDSHIP AND ENMITY	23
SCIENCE, TRUTH, RELIGION AND FALSEHOOD	24
PROPERTY AND POVERTY	25
ART AND NATURE	26
ARTIFICE AND SINCERITY	27
LIFE	28
MODERNITY AND THE AGE	29
THE ARTIST AND HIS PUBLIC	30
STYLE	31
CRITICS AND CRITICISM	32
EGOISM	32
YOUTH	33
DANDYISM	33
SOME AUTHORS	34
MODELS AND PAINTING	35

PERSONALITIES	36
EXPLOSIVES	37
LAW AND PUNISHMENT	37
VARIA	38
Anecdotes and Sayings	45
SOURCES OF THE EXTRACTS	51

COMPILER'S PREFACE

THERE IS A GOOD precedent for a little book of this sort since it follows the author's own example. On 17 August 1894, Wilde sent a telegram from Worthing to his publishers Elkin Mathews and John Lane: "My wife is compiling a small anthology of phrases from my work. You will have no objection I hope to her quoting from my plays." The publishers having "no objection whatever," the work duly appeared in the January of 1895 under the title of *Oscariana*. The first edition contained fifty copies but was followed in May of that year by a further edition of two hundred.

That Wilde himself attached importance to this work can be seen by a letter he wrote to its publisher Arthur L. Humphreys (himself an author and bookseller and for many years head of Hatchards bookshop in Piccadilly) in late November 1894. Obviously displeased with the selection as it then stood ("the plays are particularly badly done. Long passages are quoted, where a single aphorism should have been extracted"), Wilde remarked that he was "writing a new set of aphorisms" and that "the book, well done, should be a really brilliant thing: no English writer has for years ever published aphorisms.... I think also it should be bound in cloth, and look dainty and nice. I don't want a 'railway bookstall' book.... After the *Green Carnation* publication [Robert Hichens' parody of Wilde], this book of 'real Oscar Wilde' should be refined and distinguished: else, it will look like a bit of journalism."

Wilde died in 1900, and in 1904 the same publisher issued a compact 222-small-page book under the title of *Sebastian Melmoth*, the name borne by Wilde during the years of his exile in France. Of the text, 131 pages were taken up with aphorisms while the rest comprised a re-printing of Wilde's *The Soul of Man under Socialism* under the title of *The Soul of Man*, the name by which Wilde wished it to be known, fifty copies of which Humphreys had published in a privately printed edition in 1895. The following year, in the U.S. there appeared a somewhat similar volume: *Epigrams and Aphorisms* edited by G. H. Sargent, John W. Luce & Co., Boston. Thus was established in his lifetime—to be consolidated after his death—the tradition of regarding Wilde as a master of the apophthegm, the maxim, the *bon mot*, the merit of which justified their separate publication as a species of literature in their own right.

Despite this, these epigrams of Wilde have received little respected study at the hands of editors as constituting a body of attitudes, a formulary of mental poses. Logan Pearsall Smith, for example, in *A Treasury of English Aphorisms* quotes eight of them, but remarks that "Oscar Wilde's paradoxes (for all their shining wit) must for the most part, be classed among the counterfeit currency of thought" —an attack, in part, perhaps answered by Richard Le Gallienne's statement that "paradox with him [Wilde] was merely Truth standing on its head to attract attention".

Certainly Wilde's exhibitionism strengthened the dismissal of critical attention, the lack of which may have been two-fold. First, the notion, long current, held sway that Wilde was incurably frivolous, a fribble of an author with nothing to say—though he said that nothing with wit and grace. Certainly, it cannot be claimed that he diligently sought to avoid this accusation. Indeed, he often fostered it. Questioned on the witness stand by Edward Carson in his case against the Marquess of Queensberry as to whether he thought his witticism "Wickedness is a myth invented by good people to account for the curious attraction of others", true or not, Wilde replied: "I rarely think that anything I write is true." "The only thing to do with good advice," he declared elsewhere, "is to pass it on"—a cavalier dismissal of that considered earnestness cultivated by the High Victorian sage. And yet, at the same time, we know that he was — somewhat in the manner of Socrates and, more still, in that of Nietsche—a stimulating teacher of youth.

Many, no doubt, would replace the word "teacher" with the term "corrupter" here; but it may be that the wisdom inherent in Wilde's wit is that belonging to an eternal opposition, "lest one good custom should corrupt the earth". This view of the writer as an inventor of established opinion has recently been put with much brilliance by the poet George Barker. "I believe the responsibility or onus of the poet," he told an international audience at a Poetry Expo held in Montreal in 1967, "is to assert and affirm the human privilege of perversity. I believe it to be his duty to remind us that even when we are right we are at perfect liberty to change our minds because it is sometimes better to be wrong. I believe the nature of the poet to be at heart anarchic." Substitute "wit" for "poet", and the statement constitutes a perfect defence for Wilde who, of course, was also a poet.

This short preface is not the place in which to insist on momentous parallels, nor would it be in keeping with the inspired levity of Wilde. Even so, Plato's notion of the crowd as "the Great Beast"—the ignorant, gross, instinctive enemy of truth—is echoed, exaggerated, parodied almost in the maxim that: "A truth ceases to be true when more than one person believes in it." Cross-examined in Court by Carson as to whether he believed this to be so, Wilde's riposte was more serious than usual: "Perfectly. That would be my metaphysical definition of truth; something so personal that the same truth could never be appreciated by two minds." The resemblance here to Kierkegaard's notion that truth is a narrow difficult defile through which only one person, "the Individual", may pass at one time, is too striking to miss. Truth, declared Kierkegaard, is in subjectivity—an encounter, a relationship, not an external fact. To view Wilde in an existentialist perspective is perhaps both new and profitable. It should also be added here that two of Wilde's commentators *have* found the gist of substantial thought in Wilde's epigrams—Desmond MacCarthy and Hesketh Pearson, between them, discovering in his winged *pensées* ideas originated or developed by George Meredith, Samuel Butler, W. B. Yeats and Sigmund Freud.

The other reason why Wilde's witticisms have not been more critically examined is perhaps because they appeared to partake of the body and spirit of his conversation. Out of its context they perhaps seemed like isolated notes or phrases from whole symphonic movements now lost. Talk, even good talk, is subject to the nature of flux, whereas the character of a maxim must be both incisive and static. Those who heard the talk of Wilde recorded their sense of its divine gymnastic, its iridescent life, its kaleidoscopic motion. "How like was his talk," recalled E. F. Benson, "to the play of a sunlit fountain! It rose in the air constantly changing its shape, but always with the hue of the rainbow on it, and almost before you could realise the outline of this jet or that, it had vanished and another sparkled where it had been, so that you could hardly remember even the moment afterwards, what exactly it was that had enchanted you." Who would ask for literature, Goethe once remarked, if good conversation were always available? With Wilde, it so plentifully was that those who heard and remembered his talk must have thought of his written maxims as but the part compared with the whole. And they were right, we may reflect, in their splendid privilege of bathing in the music of a marvellous mind. "Who cared so long as the Pied Piper continued to flute?" To us, less fortunate, far from that voice with its "cadenced and varied intonation, pausing on a word, a sentence, as a violinist accents and phrases his music", there remains the *disjecta membra* of those moments—the *mots* and maxims of his writings which he so often rehearsed in speech, along with the *obiter dicta* recorded in anecdotes by admirers and friends. The purpose of this little collection is to bring the reader some of both of these.

* * *

In preparing this small bouquet, I have drawn from the assorted blooms of wit in all the varied borders of Wilde's spacious garden. Prominent representation has been given to the three sets of aphorisms to which he accorded separate publication: *A Preface to Dorian Gray* published in *The Fortnightly Review* in March 1890, *A Few Maxims for the Instruction of the Over-Educated* in the *Saturday Review*, 17 November 1894, and *Phrases and Philosophies for the Use of the Young* in the first issue of an Oxford undergraduate magazine *Chameleon*, December 1894. The second of these (nineteen in number) appeared anonymously; but in a letter to Arthur L. Humphreys written in the late November of 1894 Wilde remarks "The *Saturday* was of course mine", so admitting to his authorship of them. Though not recorded by Stuart Mason in his *Bibliography of Oscar Wilde* and never included in the Wilde canon, that fine scholar of the period Sir Rupert Hart-Davis assures us that "they certainly belong there". Due inclusion has also been given to those opinions of Wilde which reveal his ebullience as a literary critic, an office in which he discharged some of his brightest shafts. Here I have a few times resorted to that extremely rare volume *Essays, Criticisms and Reviews*—a collection from *Woman's World* (edited by him between 1887 and 1889 and privately printed in 1901). For the sake of inclusiveness, I have also inserted one or two aphorisms from his verse among these prose maxims of Wilde.

Recordings of his wit by others will be found under the heading *Anecdotes and Sayings* in a section at the end of this collection. These *mots* have been arranged largely in chronological order, so that their sequence, indicated by the captions in italics, constitutes a kind of epigrammatic autobiography.

The main body of witticisms (entered under *The Written Word*), I have located in groups, according to their subject or theme. The source of each maxim in this volume is given by an appended number which can be referred to in the numerical List of Extracts at the end.

Finally, I should like to thank Dr. Isabel Murray of Aberdeen University who—with her fine knowledge of Wilde—helped me generously in the compilation of this little book; leaving me only to acknowledge personally any imperfections which it might bear.

DEREK STANFORD
SEAFORD,
SUSSEX.

I summed up all systems in a phrase, and all existence in an epigram.

WILDE.

It was natural to Wilde to be artificial ... and that is why he was suspected of insincerity.

ROBERT ROSS.

His wit is often wisdom.

WILFRED LEADMAN.

THE WRITTEN WORD

VICE, SIN AND VIRTUE

[1] Wickedness is a myth invented by good people to account for the curious attractiveness of others.

[2] Good resolutions are useless attempts to interfere with scientific laws. They are simply cheques that men draw on a bank where they have no account.

[3] What is termed Sin is an essential element in progress . . . by its curiosity Sin increases the experience of the race.

[4] People are so fond of giving away what they do not want themselves that charity is largely on the increase.

[5] One can always be kind to people about whom one cares nothing.

[6] Vice and virtue are to the artist materials for an art.

[7] Pleasure is Nature's test, her sign of approval. When we are happy we are always good, but when we are good we are not always happy.

[8] A bad man is the sort of man who admires innocence.

[9] Philanthropy is the refuge of people who wish to annoy their fellow creatures.

[10] Nothing looks so like innocence as an indiscretion.

[11] Duty is what one expects from others—it is not what one does oneself.

[12] The reason we all like to think so well of others is that we are all afraid for ourselves. The basis of optimism is sheer terror.

[13] Conscience . . . is a sign of our imperfect development.

[14] To humility there is nothing that is impossible.

[15] The gods are strange. It is not our vices only they make instruments to scourge us. They bring us to ruin through what in us is good, gentle, humane, loving.

[16] The supreme vice is shallowness.

[17] One should be thankful that there is any fault of which one can be unjustly accused.

[18] The greatest sins of the world take place in the brain.

[19] The sick do not ask if the hand that smoothes their pillow is pure, nor the dying care if the lips that touch their brow have known the kiss of sin.

[20] Disobedience, in the eyes of anyone who has read history, is man's original virtue.

[21] Men become old, but they never become good.

[22] Misfortunes one can endure—they come from outside. . . . But to suffer for one's own faults—ah!—there is the sting of life.

[23] As soon as people are old enough to know better, they don't know anything at all.

WOMEN AND MARRIAGE

[24] Women represent the triumph of matter over mind, just as men represent the triumph of mind over morals.

[25] Men marry because they are tired; women because they are curious; both are disappointed.

[26] Women have a much better time than men in this world; there are more things forbidden them.

[27] The real drawback to marriage is that it makes one unselfish. And unselfish people are colourless. They lack individuality.

[28] Women as a sex are Sphinxes without secrets.

[29] Most women are so artificial that they have no sense of Art. Most men are so natural that they have no sense of Beauty.

[30] Women love us for our defects. If we have enough of them they will forgive us everything.

[31] When a woman marries again it is because she detested her first husband. When a man marries again, it is because he adored his first wife. Women try their luck; men risk theirs.

[32] Women are not meant to be judges, but to forgive us when we need forgiveness. Pardon, not punishment, is their mission.

[33] It is the feet of clay that makes the gold of the image precious.

[34] There is only one real tragedy in a woman's life. The fact that her past is always her lover, and her future invariably her husband.

[35] If a woman can't make her mistakes charming, she is only a female.

[36] More women grow old nowadays through the faithfulness of their admirers than through anything else!

[37] Every woman is a rebel, and usually in wild revolt against herself.

[38] The history of women is the history of the worst tyranny the world has ever known. The tyranny of the weak over the strong. It is the only tyranny that lasts.

[39] There's nothing in the world like the devotion of a married woman. It's a thing no married man knows anything about.

[40] No woman should ever be quite accurate about her age. It looks so calculating.

[41] If a woman really repents, she never wishes to return to the society that has made or seen her ruin.

[42] It's much too dangerous . . . for a husband to pay any attention to his wife in public. It always makes people think that he beats her when they're alone.

LOVE, FRIENDSHIP AND ENMITY

[43] Friendship is far more tragic than love. It lasts longer.

[44] A man cannot be too careful in the choice of his enemies.

[45] An acquaintance that begins with a compliment is sure to develop into a real friendship. It starts in the right manner.

[46] Yet each man kills the thing he loves,
 By each let this be heard,
Some do it with a bitter look,
 Some with a flattering word,

> The coward does it with a kiss,
> The brave man with a sword!

[47] It is very romantic to be in love. But there is nothing romantic about a definite proposal.... One may be accepted.... Then the excitement is all over. The very essence of romance is uncertainty.

SCIENCE, TRUTH, RELIGION AND FALSEHOOD

[48] Religions die when they are proved to be true. Science is a record of dead religions.

[49] Agnosticism should have its ritual no less than faith.

[50] Ours [the C. of E.] is the only Church where the sceptic stands at the altar, and where St. Thomas is regarded as the ideal apostle.

[51] The English are always degrading truths into facts. When a truth becomes a fact it loses all intellectual value.

[52] If one tells the truth, one is sure, sooner or later, to be found out.

[53] The aim of the liar is simply to charm, to delight, to give pleasure.

[54] The truth is rarely pure and never simple.

PROPERTY AND POVERTY

[55] There is only one class in the community that thinks more about money than the rich, and that is the poor. The poor can think of nothing else. That is the misery of being poor.

[56] To recommend thrift to the poor is both grotesque and insulting. It is like advising a man who is starving to eat less.

[57] If property had simply pleasures, we could stand it; but its duties make it unbearable. In the interests of the rich we must get rid of it.

[58] The real tragedy of the poor is that they can afford nothing but self-denial.

[59] It is a sad fact, but there is no doubt that the poor are completely unconscious of their own picturesqueness.

[60] The only thing that can console one for being poor is extravagance. The only thing that can console one for being rich is economy.

[61] In war the strong make slaves of the weak, and in peace the rich make slaves of the poor.

ART AND NATURE

[62] A really well-made buttonhole is the only link between Art and Nature.

[63] Art is the only serious thing in the world. And the artist is the only person who is never serious.

[64] It seems to me that we all look at Nature too much, and live with her too little.

[65] In art as in life the law of heredity holds good. *On est toujours fils de quelqu'un.*

[66] One touch of Nature makes the whole world kin, but two touches of Nature will destroy any work of Art.

[67] Lying, the telling of beautiful untrue things, is the proper aim of Art.

[68] Nature is always behind the age. It takes a great artist to be thoroughly modern.

[69] All art is at once surface and symbol. Those who go beneath the surface do so at their peril. Those who read the symbol do so at their peril.

[70] Art only begins where imitation ends.

[71] The object of art is not simple truth but complex beauty.

[72] Lounging in the open air is not a bad school for poets, but it largely depends on the lounger.

[73] There are two ways of misunderstanding a poem. One is to misunderstand it and the other to praise it for qualities it does not possess.

[74] It is always a pleasure to come across an American poet who is not national, and who tries to give expression to the literature that he loves rather than to the land in which he lives. The Muses care so little for geography!

[75] There is indeed a poetical attitude to be adopted towards all things, but all things are not fit subjects for poetry.

[76] What is abnormal in Life stands in normal relations to Art. It is the only thing in Life that stands in normal relations to Art.

[77] The world is a stage, but the play is badly cast.

ARTIFICE AND SINCERITY

[78] The first duty in life is to be as artificial as possible. What the second duty is no one has as yet discovered.

[79] A mask tells us more than a face.

[80] The fact of a man being a poisoner is nothing against his prose.

[81] All bad poetry springs from genuine feeling.

[82] To be intelligible is to be found out.

LIFE

[83] Life is a *mauvais quart d'heure* made up of exquisite moments.

[84] When a man says he has exhausted life one always knows life has exhausted him.

[85] Life imitates Art far more than Art imitates Life.

[86] When a man acts he is a puppet. When he describes he is a poet.

[87] Life is terribly deficient in form. Its catastrophes happen in the wrong way and to the wrong people. There is a grotesque horror about its comedies, and its tragedies seem to culminate in farce.

[88] All trials are trials for one's life, just as all sentences are sentences of death.

[89] . . . he who lives more lives than one
More deaths than one must die.

[90] To most of us the real life is the life we do not lead.

MODERNITY AND THE AGE

[91] Nothing is so dangerous as being too modern; one is apt to grow old-fashioned quite suddenly.

[92] I cannot but be conscious we are born in an age when the dull are treated seriously, and I live in terror of not being misunderstood.

[93] To be really mediaeval one should have no body. To be really modern one should have no soul. To be really Greek one should have no clothes.

[94] Nowadays most people die of a sort of creeping common sense, and discover when it is too late that the only things one never regrets are one's mistakes.

[95] We call ours a utilitarian age, and we do not know the uses of any single thing. We have forgotten that water can cleanse, and fire purify, and that the Earth is mother to us all.

[96] In old days nobody pretended to be a bit better than his neighbours. In fact, to be a bit better than one's neighbour was considered excessively vulgar and middle class. Nowadays, with our modern mania for morality, everyone has to pose as a paragon of purity,

incorruptibility—and all the other seven deadly virtues.

[97] Perhaps in this century we are too altruistic to be really artistic.

THE ARTIST AND HIS PUBLIC

[98] To reveal art and conceal the artist is art's aim.

[99] The public is wonderfully tolerant. It forgives everything except genius.

[100] The only thing that the artist cannot see is the obvious. The only thing that the public can see is the obvious. The result is the Criticism of the Journalist.

[101] No artist has ethical sympathies. An ethical sympathy in an artist is an unpardonable mannerism of style.

[102] Art should never try to be popular. The public should try to make itself artistic.

[103] A subject that is beautiful in itself gives no suggestion to the artist. It lacks imperfection.

[104] Public opinion exists only where there are no ideas.

[105] To disagree with three-fourths of the

British public on all points is one of the first elements of sanity, one of the deepest consolations in all moments of spiritual doubt.

[106] For him [the poet] there is but one time, the artistic moment; but one law, the law of form; but one land, the land of Beauty.

[107] If you ask nine-tenths of the British public what is the meaning of the word aesthetics, they will tell you it is the French for affectation or the German for a dado.

[108] The sign of a Philistine age is the cry of immorality against art.

[109] One who is an emperor or king may stoop down and pick up a brush for a painter; but when the democracy stoops down it is merely to throw mud.

STYLE

[110] In all unimportant matters, style, not sincerity, is the essential. In all important matters, style, not sincerity is the essential.

[111] There seems to be some curious connection between piety and poor rhymes.

[112] A simile committing suicide is always a depressing spectacle.

CRITICS AND CRITICISM

[113] The highest, as the lowest, form of criticism is a mode of autobiography.

[114] Mediocre critics are usually safe in their generalities; it is in their reasons and examples that they come so lamentably to grief.

[115] The primary aim of the critic is to see the object as in itself it really is not.

[116] The highest criticism is the record of one's own soul. It is more interesting than history, as it is concerned simply with oneself.

[117] All premature panegyrics bring their own punishment upon themselves.

[118] The first step in aesthetic criticism is to realize one's own impressions.

EGOISM

[119] To love oneself is the beginning of a life-long romance.

[120] Conscience makes egoists of us all.

[121] Selfishness is not living as one wishes to live. It is asking other people to live as one wishes to live.

[122] I am the only person in the world I should like to know thoroughly, but I don't see any chance of it just at present.

YOUTH

[123] There is nothing like youth. The middle-aged are mortgaged to Life. The old are in Life's lumber room. But youth is the Lord of Life.

[124] Those whom the gods love grow young.

[125] The old believe everything: the middle-aged suspect everything: the young know everything.

DANDYISM

[126] The future belongs to the dandy. It is the exquisites who are going to rule.

[127] The only way to atone for being occasionally a little over-dressed is by being always absolutely over-educated.

[128] Dandyism is the assertion of the absolute modernity of Beauty.

[129] A well-tied tie is the first serious step in life.

SOME AUTHORS

[130] A steady course of Balzac reduces our living friends to shadows, and our acquaintances to the shadows of shades.

[131] Meredith is a prose Browning, and so is Browning. He used poetry as a medium for writing in prose.

[132] Ah! Meredith! Who can define him? His style is chaos illuminated by flashes of lightning. As a writer he has mastered everything except language; as a novelist he can do everything, except tell a story: as an artist he is everything except articulate.

[133] André Gide's book *Les Nourritures Terrestres*, 1897 is, of course, and always has been to me, the primal and ultimate note of modern art, but *to be an Egoist one must have an Ego*. It is not everyone who says 'I,' who can enter into the Kingdom of Art.

[134] In his very rejection of art Walt Whitman is an artist.... If Poetry has passed him by, Philosophy will take note of him.

[135] He [W. E. Henley] is made to sing along the highways, not to sit down and write. If he took himself more seriously, his work would become trivial.

[136] Mr. [Walter] Pater is an intellectual

impressionist.... He has taken the sensationalism of Greek philosophy and made it a new method of art criticism.

MODELS AND PAINTING

[137] For an artist to marry his model is as fatal as for a gourmet to marry his cook: the one gets no sittings, and the other gets no dinners.

[138] They [models] are extremely good-natured and very accommodating. "What do you sit for?" said a young artist to a model who had sent him in her card.... "Oh, for anything you like, sir," said the girl, "landscape if necessary!"

[139] A beautiful model who had sat for two years to one of our most distinguished English painters, got engaged to a street vendor of penny ices. On her marriage the painter sent her a pretty wedding present, and received in return a nice letter of thanks with the following remarkable postscript: "Never eat the green ices!"

[140] To paint what you see is a good rule in art, but to see what is worth painting is better. See life under pictorial conditions. It

is better to live in a city of changeable weather than in a city of lovely surroundings.
[141] What is a picture? Primarily, a picture is a beautiful coloured surface, merely, with no more spiritual message or meaning for you than an exquisite fragment of Venetian glass or a blue tile from the wall of Damascus.

PERSONALITIES

[142] He [W. E. Henley] made his scrofula into *vers libre*, and is furious because I have made a sonnet out of 'skilly'. Besides, there are only two forms of writers in England, the unread and the unreadable. Henley belongs to the former class.
[143] He [the publisher Leonard Smithers] loves first editions especially of women.
[144] You [Leonard Smithers] are so accustomed to bringing out books limited to an edition of three copies, one for the author, one for yourself, and one for the Police, that I feel you are sinking beneath your standard in producing a sixpenny edition of anything.
[145] Frank Harris has no feelings. It is the secret of his success. Just as the fact that he

thinks that other people have none either is the secret of the failure that lies in wait for him somewhere on the way of Life.

EXPLOSIVES

[146] Explosive clocks are not very good things for foreign exportation, as, even if they succeed in passing the Custom House, the train service is so irregular, that they usually go off before they have reached their proper destination.

[147] Everything is so adulterated nowadays that even dynamite can hardly be got in a pure condition.

LAW AND PUNISHMENT

[148]

I know not whether Laws be right
   Or whether Laws be wrong;
All that we know who lie in gaol
   Is that the wall is strong;
And that each day is like a year,
   A year whose days are long.

But this I know, that every Law
   That men have made for Man
Since first Man took his brother's life,
   And the sad world began,
But straws the wheat and saves the chaff
   With a most evil fan.

This too I know—and wise it were
   If each could know the same—
That every prison that men build
   Is built with bricks of shame,
And bound with bars lest Christ should see
   How men their brothers maim.

With bars they blur the gracious moon,
   And blind the goodly sun:
And they do well to hide this Hell,
   For in it things are done
That Son of God nor son of Man
   Ever should look upon!

VARIA

History
[149] The one duty we owe to history is to re-write it.

Seriousness
[150] Dullness is the coming of age of seriousness.

Society
[151] To be in it is merely a bore. But to be out of it simply a tragedy.

Novels
[152] One should not be too severe on English novels: they are only the relaxation of the intellectually unemployed.

Novelists
[153] The difficulty under which the novelists of our day labour seems to me to be this: if they do not go into society, their books are unreadable; and if they do go into society, they have no time left for writing.

Actors
[154] We are sorry to find an English dramatic critic misquoting Shakespeare, as we had always been of the opinion that this was a privilege reserved specially for our English actors.

Pleasure
[155] Pleasure is the only thing one should live for. Nothing ages like happiness.

Ambition
[156] Ambition is the last refuge of the failure.

Contradiction
[157] The well-bred contradict other people. The wise contradict themselves.

Biography
[158] Every great man nowadays has his disciples, and it is usually Judas who writes the biography.

Christ
[159] His morality is all sympathy, just what morality should be. . . . His justice is all poetical justice, exactly what justice should be.

Memory
[160] Memory in a woman is the beginning of dowdiness.

The Cynic
[161] A cynic is a man who knows the price of everything, and the value of nothing.

The Sentimentalist
[162] The sentimentalist is always a cynic at heart. Indeed sentimentality is merely the bank-holiday of cynicism.

Optimism
[163] If you pretend to be good, the world takes you very seriously. If you pretend to be bad, it doesn't. Such is the astounding stupidity of optimism.

Common Sense
[164] Anybody can have common sense, provided that they have no imagination.

Culture
[165] More than half of modern culture depends on what one shouldn't read.

Experience
[166] Experience is the name everyone gives to their mistakes.

Labour
[167] Hard work is simply the refuge of people who have nothing whatever to do.

Romance
[168] When one is in love, one always begins by deceiving oneself, and one always ends by deceiving others. That is what the world calls a romance.

The Peerage
[169] It is the one book a young man about town should know thoroughly, and it is the

best thing in fiction the English have ever done.

Fiction
[170] The good end happily, and the bad end unhappily. That is what fiction means.

Compliments
[171] Nowadays we are all of us so hard up, that the only pleasant things to pay are compliments.

Candour
[172] Whenever one has anything unpleasant to say, one should always be quite candid.

Tears
[173] Crying is the refuge of plain women but the ruin of pretty ones.

Good People
[174] Good people do a great deal of harm in this world . . . they make badness of such extraordinary importance.

Platitudes
[175] In modern life nothing produces such an effect as a platitude. It makes the whole world kin.

Pessimism
[176] Optimism begins in a broad grin, and Pessimism ends with blue spectacles.

Fair Play
[177] One should always play fairly . . . when one has the winning cards.

Parliament
[178] The Lords Temporal say nothing, the Lords Spiritual have nothing to say, and the House of Commons has nothing to say and says it.

ANECDOTES AND SAYINGS

Oscar at Oxford
[179] "I hope I shall be able to live up to my blue china."

"Professor of Aesthetics"
[180] He arrived late at lunch one day, and the hostess reproved him with a glance at the clock. "And what do you think the little clock knows of what the great golden sun is doing?" he asked her.

[181] Mrs. Langtry [the Jersey Lily] "owes it to herself to drive through Hyde Park in a black Victoria drawn by black horses and with 'Venus Annodomini' emblazoned on her black bonnet in dull sapphires. But she won't."

Oscar in America
[182] "Have you anything to declare?" asked the customs official. "No, I have nothing to declare;" he paused: "except my genius."

[183] "I am not exactly pleased with the Atlantic," he told the reporters. "It is not so majestic as I expected."

[184] He was even unimpressed by the Niagara Falls, which he described as "simply

a vast unnecessary amount of water going the wrong way and then falling over unnecessary rocks."

[185] "Give children beauty, not the record of bloody slaughters and barbarous brawls, as they call history, or of the latitude and longitude of places nobody cares about, as they call geography."

[186] "Caricature is the tribute which mediocrity pays to genius."

[187] "And how much are you paid for the stupid things you have said about me?" Oscar asked a young reporter. "Six dollars," he replied. "Well, the rate for lying is not very high in America."

[188] To the journalists who awaited him [on his return] at Liverpool, Oscar remarked: "The English and Americans have everything in common, except, of course, their language."

Oscar in Paris
[189] "The Oscar of the first period is now dead. We are now concerned with the Oscar of the second period, who has nothing in common with the gentleman who wore long hair and carried a sunflower down Piccadilly."

[190] "I am having my hair curled that I may resemble Nero."

[191] During his continual pursuit of celebrities, Oscar had met Coquelin; he made a note of his conversation with the actor. "What is civilization, Mr. Wilde?" "Love of beauty." "And what is beauty?" "That which the middle classes call ugly." "And what do the middle classes call beauty?" "It does not exist."

"Amiable ... esurient Oscar"

[192] When he was thirty, Oscar said to a friend, "My name has two 'O's, two 'F's, and two 'W's. A name which is destined to be in everyone's mouth must not be too long. It comes too expensive in the advertisement. When one is unknown a number of Christian names are useful, perhaps needful. As one becomes famous one sheds some of them, just as a balloonist, when rising higher, sheds unnecessary ballast. All but two of my five names have already been thrown overboard. Soon I shall discard another and be known as "The Wilde" or "The Oscar."

[193] "The man who can dominate a London dinner-table can dominate the world."

[194] "Missionaries, my dear," I remember Wilde once saying at a dinner party. "Don't you realize that missionaries are the divinely

provided food for destitute and underfed cannibals."

[195] "Twenty years of romance make a woman look like a ruin; but twenty years of marriage make her something like a public building."

[196] "Work is the curse of the drinking classes."

[197] "It is personalities, not principles, that rule the age."

[198] Once when [Frank] Harris spoke too often of his own social success and of all the great houses he had visited, Oscar remarked: "Yes, dear Frank, we believe you—you have dined in every house in London—*once*."

[199] Wilde carried his transmutation of values to mania; if he did not like a name he altered it or mispronounced . . . Arthur Symons' name, for some reason I could never grasp, he persistently mispronounced, calling him Simons, with the i long. "But he calls himself Simmons," I said. "How can he be so foolish! It is perfectly clear that Symons doesn't know how to pronounce his own name."

[200] "The gods bestowed on Max [Beerbohm] the gift of perpetual old age."

[201] Asked what he thought of [Bernard] Shaw, Wilde replied "Shaw has not an enemy in the world, and none of his friends like him."

[202] "I know [George] Moore so well that I have not spoken to him for ten years."

[203] "The basis of literary friendship is mixing the poisoned bowl."

Pride and Downfall

[204] To a remark of Bernard Berenson, he replied "Bernard, you forget that in every way I want to imitate my Maker and, like Him, I want nothing but praise."

[205] "Have you noticed how annoyed pigs become if you do not cast pearls before them?"

[206] "Would you like to know the great drama of my life. It is that I have put my genius into my life—I have put only my talents into my work."

[207] [André Gide wrote that] Nietzsche surprised me less, on a later occasion because I had heard Wilde say, "No, not happiness! Certainly not happiness! Pleasure. One must always set one's heart upon the most tragic."

Oscar on Trial

[208] "My poor brother writes to me that he is defending me all over London; my poor,

dear brother, he would compromise a steam engine."

[209] On the second day of the trial, Oscar met a friend of his called Charles Goodhard in Piccadilly Circus. Oscar was in high spirits, and Goodhard did not like to touch on the subject ... but Oscar said, "You've heard of my case, I suppose?" "Oh—er—yes," replied Goodhard nervously. "I'm sure I wish you the best of luck—er." Oscar spared his feelings. "Don't distress yourself. All is well. The working classes are with me—to a boy."

Oscar in Exile

[210] "When I was a boy my two favourite characters were Lucien de Rubempré and Julien Sorel. Lucien hanged himself. Julien died on the scaffold, and I died in prison."

[211] "I have made an important discovery —that alcohol taken in sufficient quantities produces all the effects of intoxication."

[212] Over the mantelpiece hung a tawdry mirror. The wall-paper was a horror of large magenta flowers: "Decidedly one of us will have to go," he said once, as he looked at it.

[213] "I am dying beyond my means."

SOURCES OF THE EXTRACTS

THE WRITTEN WORD

A Critic in Pall Mall (Ed. Robert Ross)
   65, 72, 73, 97, 111, 112, 114, 117, 134, 135, 136, 152, 153, 154.

A Few Maxims for the Instruction of the Over-Educated
   29, 43, 51, 60, 63, 76, 93, 100, 103, 104.

A House of Pomegranates
   61.

A Woman of No Importance
   8, 11, 19, 26, 28, 37, 38, 83, 84, 126, 129, 151, 160, 165, 167.

An Ideal Husband
   9, 32, 34, 36, 45, 91, 96, 175, 176, 177.

De Profundis
   14, 15, 16, 17, 18, 49, 64, 70, 88, 95, 159, 162.

Essays & Lectures (Ed. Robert Ross)
   59, 75, 90, 105, 106, 107, 108, 137, 138, 139, 140, 141.

Essays, Criticisms and Reviews (privately printed)
  4, 68, 79.

Intentions
  3, 13, 50, 53, 66, 67, 71, 79, 80, 81, 85, 86, 87, 92, 99, 115, 116, 118, 122, 130, 131, 132, 133, 149.

Lady Windermere's Fan
  10, 21, 22, 23, 39, 41, 42, 82, 161, 163, 166, 171, 173, 174.

Lord Arthur Saville's Crime and Other Stories
  35, 77, 146, 147.

Phrases and Philosophies for the Use of the Young
  48, 52, 62, 78, 109, 119, 125, 127, 150, 155, 156, 157.

The Artist as Critic: Critical Writings of Oscar Wilde (Ed. Richard Ellmann)
  158.

The Ballad of Reading Gaol
  46, 89, 148.

The Happy Prince and Other Tales
  164, 167.

The Importance of Being Earnest
   40, 47, 54, 170, 172.

The letters of Oscar Wilde (Ed. Rupert Hart-Davis)
   133, 142, 143, 144, 145.

The Picture of Dorian Gray
   2, 5, 6, 7, 12, 24, 25, 27, 30, 31, 33, 44, 58, 69, 94, 98, 101, 113, 120, 123, 168.

The Soul of Man under Socialism
   30, 55, 56, 57, 102, 109, 121, 178.

ANECDOTES AND SAYINGS

Aspects of Oscar Wilde by Vincent O'Sullivan
   199, 200, 210.

Autobiographies by W. B. Yeats
   190, 203, 208.

Oscar Wilde by Philippe Jullian
   181, 186, 187, 188, 189, 191, 192, 198, 201, 202, 209, 211, 212.

Oscar Wilde by G. J. Renier
   179, 180, 183, 213.

Oscar Wilde—A Study by André Gide
206, 207.

Recollections of Oscar Wilde by Charles Ricketts
205.

Sunset and Twilight by Bernard Berenson
204.

The Eighteen-Nineties by Holbrook Jackson
193, 197.

The Life of Oscar Wilde by Hesketh Pearson
182, 184, 185, 195, 196.

The Romantic Nineties by Richard Le Gallienne.
194.

WARNER MEMORIAL LIBRARY
EASTERN COLLEGE
ST. DAVIDS, PA. 19087

PR 5812 .S65
Wilde, Oscar, 1854-1900.
Witticisms of Oscar Wilde;